THE TAXI PROJECT

THE TAXI PROJECT

EMMA ARI BELTRAN

MARTHA KUWEE KUMSA

SHENG XUE

GORAN SIMIC

The TAXI Project
first published 2010 by
Scirocco Drama
An imprint of J. Gordon Shillingford Publishing Inc.

Scirocco Drama Editor: Glenda MacFarlane
Cover design by Terry Gallagher / Doowah Design Inc.
Production photos by Alex Felipe
Printed and bound in Canada on 100% post-consumer recycled paper.

We acknowledge the financial support of the Manitoba Arts Council, The Canada Council for the Arts and the Government of Canada through the Book Publishing Industry Development Program (BPIDP) for our publishing program.

Production inquiries should be addressed to:
Josh Bloch
416-562-0982
jbloch@arcfest.org

Library and Archives Canada Cataloguing in Publication

The TAXI project / Emma Ari Beltrán… [et al.].

A play.
ISBN 978-1-897289-47-1

1. Immigrants—Canada—Drama. I. Beltrán, Emma Ari.

PS8600.T39 2010 C812'.6 C2010-901726-9

J. Gordon Shillingford Publishing
P.O. Box 86, RPO Corydon Avenue, Winnipeg, MB Canada R3M 3S3

Dedicated to the victims and survivors of the Tiananmen Square Uprising, the Red Terror, the Universidad Nacional Autónoma de México student protests, and the Bosnian War.

Acknowledgments

Benjamin Santamaria Ochoa, Anand Rajaram, Paula Rivera, and all the members of the Writers in Exile Program at PEN Canada for their contribution and support of this initiative.

The Origins of *The Taxi Project*

The TAXI Project was conceived as an arts-based initiative by PEN Canada and the Art for Real Change Collective that began in 2006. The project aimed to engage communities across Canada in a creative exploration of freedom of expression, exile and refugee experiences.

At the core of the initiative was a theatrical production. The play is a collective creation based on the lives and writings of four members of PEN Canada's Writers in Exile Program: Emma Ari Beltrán, Martha Kuwee Kumsa, Goran Simic and Sheng Xue. The Writers in Exile Program is a network of writers living in Canada from around the world forced to leave their home countries because they were unable to write freely.

The play was developed over the course of three years, weaving together the experiences of four writers from diverse literary, political, cultural, and linguistic backgrounds. This development process was supported by theatre artists Weyni Mengesha, Erica Kopyto, and Josh Bloch. The creation of the text came from varied processes. Some text in the play originates from works already published by the writers—much of the poetry for example. Some scenes were written collaboratively by the creative team. The character of Seeyyee Sera is almost entirely based on the piece "Home and Exile" by Martha Kuwee Kumsa as well as some biographical interviews that were conducted with the writer. Some scenes began as mere concepts and were translated into movement or rhythmic pieces with actors by director Weyni Mengesha.

The TAXI Project was part of a larger initiative, which also included various public staged readings, workshops, artistic showcases, presentations in public schools, the commissioning of a documentary film on youth and freedom of expression, collaborations with social justice organizations, and speaking engagements by writers living in exile in Canada.

Production Notes

The TAXI Project playwrights come from varied writing traditions. Although all accomplished professional writers, they come from journalism, theatre, poetic and academic disciplines. The play incorporates works from these diverse literary styles not originally intended for the theatre.

The play also included extra-textual devices such as music, sound, projected images, and documentary images that reflect the different cultures, and complex political events in the play.

The main characters in the play are based on the lives and writings of the participating playwrights. Some scenes are very true to actual experiences while others depart from the writers' experiences. In this sense, the characters should not be considered as biographical representations of the writers.

The play was conceived as a show that would tour to high schools and non-theatrical spaces.

Production History

The TAXI Project was produced by PEN Canada and the Art for Real Change Collective in July, 2008, at The Alchemy Theatre, Toronto, with the following cast and crew:

SEEYYEE Sera .... Miranda Edwards

EXYOU Peric .... Patrick Garrow

ALEJANDRA Pineda .... Mayahuel Tecozautla

Zhang XIAO HONG .... Diana Tso

Directed by Weyni Mengesha

Produced by Josh Bloch

Dramaturg: Erica Kopyto

Lighting Design by Gillian Wolpert

Video Design by Simon Clemo

Sound Design by Thomas Payne

Set and Costume Design by Jackie Chau

Stage Manager: Chris Humphrey

Associate Dramaturg: Marjorie Chan

Creative Development and Outreach: Anjula Gogia

Lead Writer in Exile: Emma Ari Beltrán

A Play for Four Actors

ALEJANDRA Pineda: A young activist from Mexico. A writer.

EXYOU Peric: A photojournalist / taxi driver / poet from Bosnia.

Zhang XIAO HONG: A journalist / activist from China.

SEEYYEE Sera: An Oromo activist from Ethiopia. An academic.

Other: Announcement, Immigration Officer, Pedestrians 1 & 2, Editor, Fang, Interrogators 1 & 2, Old Woman, Soldier, Emcee, Baby Brother.

Off-Stage Voices: Radio, Michelle, Friends 1 & 2, Army Officer Voice.

About the Authors

Emma Ari Beltrán is a poet from Mexico. Since 1994, she has been involved in the struggle of indigenous peoples facilitating poetry and popular theatre workshops for women and children throughout Mexico. Beltrán was a founding member of the first community radio station in Mexico's history during the student strike at the National Autonomous University of Mexico in 1999. This work caused her to be subject to political charges, kidnapping and torture, by the Mexican National Army (March 2001). Exiled in Canada since May 2002, Beltrán's poetry has been published in various literary journals and anthologies.

Sheng Xue grew up in Beijing and moved to Canada soon after the Tiananmen Square massacre in 1989. In 2000, she won the Canadian Association of Journalists Award for Investigative Journalism and the National Magazine Award. In 2001, Sheng Xue investigated China's most prominent smuggling case and published the book *Unveiling the Yuan Hua Case,* which created shock waves both inside and outside China. Her poetry collection book *Seeking the Soul of Snow* was banned by Chinese authorities banned the book before it was published in Feb. 2007.

Goran Simic was born in Bosnia and has published many volumes of poetry, drama and short fiction and librettos for opera. His work has been translated into more than ten languages and published and performed in several European countries. One of the most prominent writers of the former Yugoslavia, Simic and his family were trapped in the siege of Sarajevo. In 1996 they were able to settle in Canada as a result of a PEN Freedom to Write Award. His poetry in translation includes the books *Sprinting from the Graveyard,* and *Immigrant Blues.* His new poetry collection *Sunrise in the eyes of the Snowman* and a short story collection *Looking for Tito* is due to be published in 2010.

Martha Kuwee Kumsa is an Oromo, born and raised in Ethiopia. She worked as a journalist there until being imprisoned early in 1980. She spent 10 years in jail and was released upon the intervention of PEN and Amnesty International. PEN Canada adopted her as an Honorary Member while she was in prison and helped bring her to Canada after her release. She was one of two scholars to join the new Scholars-at-Risk Program at University of Toronto's Massey College. Pursuing a career change, Martha studied for her PhD at the Faculty of Social Work, U of T. She is currently teaching at the Faculty of Social Work, Wilfrid Laurier University.

(l to r): Miranda Edwards (Seeyee), Mayahuel Tecozautla (Alejandra), Patrick Garrow (Exyou) and Diana Tso (Xiao Hong).

Scene 1: Arrival

Toronto's Pearson International Airport. A cacophony of airport sounds. Characters move through the scene like a dance. ANNOUNCEMENT and IMMIGRATION OFFICER are spoken by all except EXYOU.

EXYOU: Please do not leave your bags unattended.

ANNOUNCEMENT: Boarding. Flight. Delayed. Report. Passenger. Cancelled. *(Words become a rhythm.)*

EXYOU: Open the Door, the guests are coming.
Some raised in the sun, some of them pale.

Every one with suitcases made of human skin.

ANNOUNCEMENT: Paging passenger Santamaria please report to Gate 6.

EXYOU: If you look carefully at the handles, fragile as birds' spines, you will find your own fingerprints, your mother's tears, your grandpa's sweat.

ANNOUNCEMENT: Flight 142 now boarding at Gate C.

EXYOU: The rain just started. The world is grey.

ANNOUNCEMENT: Due to new security measures, all bags left unattended will immediately be removed from the premises.

EXYOU: The guests are coming.

Some of them happy, some of them strange, with stomachs already full of strange words they have

just learned, like river and wheat.
Instead of food they still eat their own memories.

ANNOUNCEMENT: Boarding. Flight. Delayed. Report. Passenger. Cancelled.

EXYOU: And they are not ringing. They just gently knock on your door not to disturb your dog still hot for a fight with a strange cat that dropped by in the backyard from who knows where.

XIAO HONG: Flight 1989 from the Tiananmen Square Massacre, China, arrived.

SEEYYEE: Flight 1978 from the Red Terror, Ethiopia...Oromia. Arrived.

ALEJANDRA: Flight 1999 from the National University student strike, Mexico, arrived.

EXYOU: Flight 1994 from the Bosnian War, Yugoslavia arrived.

Flight 1 from Burma arrived—

SEEYYEE: Flight 2 from Sudan arrived—

ALEJANDRA: Flight 3 from Vietnam arrived—

XIAO HONG: Flight 4 from South Africa arrived—

EXYOU: Flight 5 from El Salvador arrived—

SEEYYEE: Flight 6 from Lebanon arrived—

ALEJANDRA: Flight 7 East Timor arrived—

XIAO HONG: Flight 8 Uganda arrived—

EXYOU: Flight 9 North Korea arrived—

SEEYYEE: Flight 10 Palestine arrived—

ALEJANDRA: Flight 11 Argentina arrived—

XIAO HONG: Flight 12 Afghanistan arrived—

EXYOU: Flight 13 Iraq arrived.

ALEJANDRA: Many more left behind.

EXYOU: The rain just started. It looks like snow.

The guests are in the house.

IMMIGRATION OFFICER: Name and Country of Origin.

ALEJANDRA: Alejandra Pineda, Mexico.

XIAO HONG: Zhang Xiao Hong, China.

EXYOU: Exyou Peric, Bosnia.

SEEYYEE: Seeyyee Sera, Ethiopia.

EXYOU: Some of them smooth as silk, some shy as a breeze.

ALEJANDRA: I only brought my journals.

SEEYYEE: I have a Masters in Sociology from the University of Addis Ababa.

XIAO HONG: Can you repeat the question?

EXYOU: Their fingers are as heavy as jail bars
while turning the leaves of your family tree.

ALEJANDRA: I could not complete school. We were on strike. I ran an independent radio station.

SEEYYEE: I was imprisoned. I gave birth to my daughter when I was there.

XIAO HONG: We wanted democracy but we got bullets.

SEEYYEE: My children. Who can I ask about my children?

EXYOU: And don't be surprised at hearing your ancestors

speak to them in some language you forgot a long time ago.

Even the dust on their shoes strangely recalls the dust in your attic.

SEEYYEE / ALEJANDRA / XIAO HONG: I am traveling alone.

EXYOU: I was a photojournalist for the Bosnian daily paper for 11 years. I taught graduate students at the University of Sarajevo.

ANNOUNCEMENT: Welcome to Canada. Bienvenue au Canada.

An envelope is passed to EXYOU. Sounds of wind are heard. It is the first time the characters have seen a Canadian winter. They huddle together. Each character tosses a handful of snow in the air. A moment of beauty as they watch it fall. Then reality. EXYOU opens up the envelope. Inside is a yellow "TAXI" sign. He places it on top of the cab.

Scene 2: Lost

A winter day. XIAO HONG is lost, having just arrived in Toronto. She has a map but can't make sense of where she is.

XIAO HONG: Excuse me.

PEDESTRIAN 1: Pardon me.

PEDESTRIAN 2: Pardon me, sorry. Excuse me.

XIAO HONG: *(To PED 2.)* Excuse me. I'm looking for…

(To PED 1.) Excuse me.

PED 1: Sorry.

XIAO HONG looks at her map again

XIAO HONG: *(To PED 2.)* Excuse me…?

PED 2: Sorry honey. I don't have any change.

XIAO HONG: No, not change…

EXYOU drives up in his taxi. The interior is covered in Polaroid portraits.

EXYOU: Do you need a taxi? It appears you are lost.

XIAO HONG: No…well…

EXYOU: What are you looking for?

XIAO HONG: A place that will give me information.

EXYOU: Are you new?

She nods her head.

EXYOU: There's a shelter. It's where I went when I first arrived.

XIAO HONG: Could you show me how to get there?

EXYOU: This place doesn't look the same when it's snowing. Let me drive you.

XIAO HONG: No. I would rather walk.

EXYOU: You know, if you have no money you are penniless but if you lost your soul you are poor. I don't think you belong to the second category. I'll drive you for free.

XIAO HONG: For free?

EXYOU: This is a city of strangers, and judging by your accent we belong to the same tribe.

She climbs in.

XIAO HONG: This is really kind of you.

EXYOU: It's my pleasure. I remember when I first came. I had a hundred and forty dollars in my pocket and my camera in an empty suitcase. But I was lucky. I came in the summer.

She notices the Polaroid pictures covering the interior of the taxicab.

XIAO HONG: Who are these people in the pictures?

EXYOU: Back home I was a photographer documenting life in my city. Now it is destroyed. These are the people of my new city.

That's Mbeki, sitting in front of the funeral home?

Once a famous disc jockey back home, he sold a great record collection to buy a ticket to the promised land. Now he's listening to painful silence broken only by coins jingling in his hat. That's Vesna walking along the strip bar street in a skirt that hides nothing. She came on the same flight I did to get married to someone she met through a pen-pal exchange. I guess it's the same tattooed bastard who is shouting from his car at her to unbutton her blouse and smile. Does he know she was once a ballerina?

That grey man crossing the street in a wheelchair, That's Ernesto.

Once a photographer, now just a frame. Obsessed with lotteries, he served for years as a lab rat renting his body for military experiments. The day he won big money he came down with a rotting illness no one had heard of before. Now, he spends his money buying deodorants to quell the stench on his way to the casino.

XIAO HONG: You have the voice of a poet.

EXYOU: I'm a better poet than a driver; I just missed your stop. Sorry, sometimes the photos overpower me.

XIAO HONG: Is it a custom to have shoes hanging from your mirror?

EXYOU: They once belonged to my son. I lost him when he was very young. See those shoes hanging there, I can see the past. As well as who is behind my car.

XIAO HONG: Your wife must be terribly sad.

EXYOU: The one who shot my son, every single post in Bosnia is decorated by his wanted poster. I spent years searching for him.

XIAO HONG: He was killed, I'm sorry.

EXYOU: Where are you from?

XIAO HONG: China. Back home we don't need wanted posters.

They arrive.

EXYOU: This is you. Call me if you need a taxi. *(He hands her his card.)* If you need more help immigrants usually meet at Salvation Army.

XIAO HONG: I don't like the word salvation.

EXYOU: I don't like the word Army.

She opens the door.

XIAO HONG: Oh, it's so cold outside. It's so cold. Thank you for the ride.

EXYOU: Wait. May I take your picture?

XIAO HONG: What is your story about me?

EXYOU: I only have a beginning

EXYOU takes a Polaroid of XIAO HONG.

XIAO HONG: Thank you.

Scene 3: Memory—Exyou in Bosnia

The Siege of Sarajevo, 1993. EXYOU enters the office of the daily paper where he works. It is in chaos. Windows are smashed, desks overturned. The EDITOR is hiding under the desk.

EDITOR: Get down. Get down. What are you still doing here? I thought you had left already.

EXYOU: They're gone... they're gone...

Bullets fly.

EDITOR: C'mon! Some crazy sniper has been trying to get into the Guinness Book of World Records for executing journalists.

EXYOU: They're gone...

EDITOR: Snap out of it Exyou. We gotta go! They'll leave without us!

EXYOU: They're gone...

EDITOR: They've killed Ivanka too! I'm taking her film. Now, let's go! I can no longer act as a gravedigger who only writes obituaries.

EXYOU: ...My son. My wife.

EDITOR: What?

More bullets.

EDITOR: Get down!! Exyou! Get down!

EXYOU: They're dead.

EDITOR: I'm so sorry.

EXYOU: Sorry…what an ugly word. Sorry. What does it mean?

Bullets.

Does it mean anything anymore in Sarajevo!

Sniper bullets hit the window. EXYOU walks towards the blown-out window.

EDITOR: Exyou, Exyou, please. I can't help you out of that minefield. Get away from there. They will kill you.

EXYOU: I have nothing.

EDITOR: I can't help you.

Bullets.

Please, I've already dragged three bodies out of here!

EXYOU: They're paying the price for the photos that I took—that you published.

EDITOR: If I thought that not publishing your photos would—

EXYOU: Would you have rejected the photos if you knew my family would be made into targets?

EDITOR: That's the risk you take when you vow to tell the truth. Hundreds of civilians were executed. Even if it was only one we must raise our voice as witnesses. We're witnesses, Exyou!

EXYOU steps away from the window. More bullets. EXYOU crouches down next to the EDITOR.

C'mon, let's go! Take your film!

EXYOU We are under siege, no one can leave.

EDITOR There is a bus convoy taking the wounded children out of the city. We'll get into the luggage compartment.

EXYOU: Like stowaways.

Bullets.

Who will bury my family?

EDITOR: We'll find a place! We have to leave now!

EXYOU: Who will bury my family? I can't leave them to rot.

EDITOR: We have to go, Exyou. The bus will leave without us!

Scene 4: Fleeing

A movement scene. The characters fleeing their home countries. A soundscape is heard of dogs barking, soldiers marching, sirens wailing, tanks rolling, and protests raging. We see images of the political events that forced the characters into exile.

We see ALEJANDRA leading a protest.

ALEJANDRA: *(Chants.)* El pueblo unido jamás será vencido. *(Translation:The people united will never be defeated.)*

Soundsofsoldiers. ALEJANDRA donsadisguise—a baseball cap. She runs. EXYOU emerges from the luggage compartment of a bus with a suitcase. He's crawling—terrified to be discovered. Sounds of dogs barking. He runs, leaving the suitcase behind. XIAO HONG emerges from inside the suitcase. She runs. Flashlights are searching for SEEYYEE. She is scrambling to find a place to hide. It is too late. There is nowhere to go. She is caught.

Scene 5: Immigration

We hear an automated voice system guiding us through an immigration application. It leads us in circles. SEEYYEE is in an immigration office in downtown Toronto.

SEEYYEE: I was released in September 1989 after a decade of torture and incarceration. Even though my imprisonment was limited to the radius of the prison compound—Ethiopia itself was a giant cell.

Life outside became stranger than when I lived behind bars. I did not have a home to go back to. Worse still, I was conscripted into the military.

If I refused conscription, I would be hunted down as a fugitive and killed. If I accepted it I would be eliminated in the training camps. It was death either way. With the "rebels" closing in from all directions, the country was coming apart and unraveling fast. It was a moment of chaos. I couldn't decipher between friends and foes. I could not trust anybody. I knew the regime was coming down fast but I did not want it to take me down with it. I decided at that point that if I had to die I would die running for dear life. I dragged my three kids out of school and ran. We hid in the bushes by the day and ran by the night. My heart skipping beats at every twist and turn and at every rustle of leaves, I wondered if I'd made the right decision taking all my children with me. What if we were caught? What if they killed us all? I had to leave them behind with my baby brother.

I had to leave my children behind, do you understand? So, please, please, can you help me? Can you help me bring my children to Canada?

Mayahuel Tecozautla (Alejandra)

Sceene 6: Memory—Ale's Interrogation

The National Autonomous University of Mexico, Mexico City. 1999. ALEJANDRA broadcasts from the students' underground radio station.

ALEJANDRA: Welcome to Que Huelga Community Radio broadcasting from inside the National Autonomous University of Mexico. We are in our 136th day of the student strike defending our right to free education and the end to the privatization of our public university. Today we have direct coverage…

The radio is interrupted by the sound of gunshots.

ARMY OFFICER VOICE: This is the National Mexican Army. Anyone occupying the campus of the National University is under arrest. Stay where you are, have your ID ready, and DO NOT try to escape, you are surrounded. I repeat, DO NOT try to escape. That is an order!

An interrogation cell. ALEJANDRA is hooded and her hands are tied up behind her back.

SOLDIER: I just want you to take a seat. I will never understand people like you: sacrificing everything for nothing! Look at your bare feet. Why would you try to escape? You knew we were going to get you. *(He rips off her hood.)* Don't worry. I am here to talk, as simple as that. So I will really appreciate if we can have an open conversation about your involvement in the "independent radio station". Which by the way was not "independent", it was totally illegal! Of course I'm not here to discuss legal minutiae.

As I said, I am here to talk. We arrested over two thousand students today, but we are missing some of the key people from your radio station. So I was hoping you could help me find them. What do you say?

ALEJANDRA does not respond.

Ah, silence is not a good choice. It might make you feel like a hero for a bit but sooner or later you will have to pay the price.

ALEJANDRA does not respond.

If you do not want to talk to me I will have to seek help from my comrades–do you like how I call them my comrades, I learned it from you. It was sort of tender seeing you take off the dust of such words:"utopia, revolution, comrades", all dressed up in black and red. Where'd you learn that?

ALEJANDRA does not respond.

My "comrades" are not as nice and well educated as your comrades. They don't believe in persuasion, they believe in electricity. So let me give you some advice…I am telling you this because you are obviously a very intelligent girl: you better start talking right now. Start talking now. Start talking. Alejandra Pineda. Alejandra Pineda…

A buzzer is heard. The soldiers voice is distorted. It becomes the voice of MICHELLE, ALEJANDRA's girlfriend in Canada. ALEJANDRA wakes up from her memory.

Scene 7: Work

A retail warehouse. ALEJANDRA is on break talking to MICHELLE on the phone.

MICHELLE: Ale? Ale? Ale? Ale?

ALEJANDRA: Huh?

MICHELLE: Babe, where'd you go?

ALEJANDRA: Nowhere. Sorry, what were you saying?

MICHELLE: I was just asking if you'll be home for dinner.

ALEJANDRA: I can't. They just asked me to close again.

MICHELLE: Oh did you ask about getting off early on Saturday?

ALEJANDRA: I forgot.

MICHELLE: Ale. It's my birthday, you promised.

ALEJANDRA: OK, OK. I gotta get back.

MICHELLE: 'Kay. I love you.

A buzzer sounds ALEJANDRA goes back to work. The characters are stacking boxes. In their short breaks, they frantically try to carry on with their lives. They lift, load, and pass boxes in a rhythmic pattern. A buzzer sounds. SEEYYEE is on break. She moves to a phone to call her children.

SEEYYEE: Hi baby, can you put your sister on the phone? Ayantu, did you take the chicken out of the freezer? Well, make sure you let it thaw properly. If your brother finishes his dinner, only then can he have dessert. Remember to check his homework—Ms. Mackenzie called again *(The buzzer sounds. SEEYYEE must go back to work)* I've got to go…

The characters are sweeping again, in a rhythmic pattern. A buzzer sounds. EXYOU is on a break. He runs to the phone. We hear the end of his conversation.

EXYOU: No I can't hold. They transferred me to you… She's my wife. She's female. Last name Peric… A young boy—age three… No I don't have the death certificates. I just want to know where they are buried… No, don't transfer me. Odjebi! *(Translation: Fuck off!)*

A buzzer sounds. EXYOU returns to work. Everyone continues sweeping. A buzzer sounds. XIAO HONG is on break. She uses the free moment to work on her articles. She speaks into a dictaphone.

XIAO HONG: On the West Chang'an Boulevard in Beijing. It is daybreak, about 6:00 A.M.—June 4th, 1989. We have just left the Tiananmen Square from the southeast corner in a peaceful and orderly fashion. I am among a large group of students marching from east to west. I am at the back of the crowd. We are the students who have taken a stand—we believe that we can make a change. We know the world is watching.

We keep to the south side of the Boulevard, in the bicycle lane. Just after we turn from west Chang'an Boulevard to Liubukou St.

An explosion is heard. An image of a tank is seen. XIAO HONG is thrown back into her memories. She is coughing.

(In Mandarin.) Wo kan bu jian, wo shen me dou kan bu jian, bang bang wo. *(Translation: I can't see, I can't see anything. I can't breathe. I can't… Help me!)*

FANG, a student, rushes to her.

FANG: Let me take you to the side of the street.

A tank approaches.

XIAO HONG: At that moment a line of tanks races towards us, traveling from east to west. With all her force, Fang pushes me out of the way towards the guardrail. The tank approaches the sidewalk and closes in on both of us. The barrel of the gun is inches from our faces. Fang falls to the ground and begins to roll. It is too late. The treads roll over her legs. She is dragged quite a distance.

I lost consciousness.

Scene 8: Writing Home

An internet café, in Toronto. SEEYYEE and ALEJANDRA are typing at computers.

SEEYYEE: Dear Baby Brother, Guess what? I got a job! I can finally leave the warehouse. It's only a part-time teaching position, just two classes a week. But, I can work on my degree at the same time! Who knows, maybe one day you can call me doctor, or professor? We're finding our ground again. We're slowly learning to live together under the same roof as mother and children. They say hello and they miss their uncle's stories. They say I don't cook the way you did. I worry when you don't write. Let me know you're OK. I've heard it's getting more dangerous. Be smart, you can only help the struggle if you stay out of prison. I should be making more money at the new job. Hopefully I'll be able to send some soon. I love you. We miss you. Big Sister.

ALEJANDRA: Dear Paloma. It's great to hear from you. I miss you and everyone very much. I'm still with the same girl, Michelle. The one I met at the rally in Quebec. She's teaching me French. Actually, we are moving in together. I think I am ready. I heard a rumour that they shut down Manuel's newspaper, is that true? Do they know about yours? Maybe you should change locations. I'm sorry I haven't sent you the poem for the new issue. It's coming, I swear. I am trying to write. It's hard to find the time and energy here. The sun sets at four! It's crazy. I haven't been sleeping well…maybe it's…just… dreams. Anyway, I'll get some poetry to you soon. Say hi to everyone from me. Ciao, au revoir, Ale.

Scene 9: Garbany

EXYOU is in his taxi. He is scanning through the radio. He stops on…

RADIO: …the good news is that tomorrow a big sale begins at Garbany Fashion House.

Believe it or not up to 50% off! *(We hear the Garbany jingle.)*

XIAO HONG enters the taxi.

EXYOU: Where to?

XIAO HONG: Pearson International Airport. *(She notices her Polaroid stuck to the interior of the taxi.)*

Hey, that's me!

EXYOU: China. Right?

XIAO HONG: You remember.

EXYOU: Just the special ones. Arrivals or departures?

XIAO HONG: Departures.

EXYOU: Are you going home?

XIAO HONG: *(Nods.)* My ma is sick.

RADIO: Our new Spring collection is now on sale with a special bonus: Every customer gets a CD with Garbany's jingle!

XIAO HONG: Can you do me a favour and turn down the radio? I've been working at the Garbany warehouse for three years.

EXYOU: No? I worked nights in that rat house for two years. It's all I could get with my Bosnian diploma. I was loading merchandise off the trucks into the warehouse.

XIAO HONG: Did you love it as much as I did?

EXYOU: Sometimes we'd laugh:"Where's Armani?" "Getting steamed in the backroom with Donna Karan."

XIAO HONG: Yeah, yeah, "What's Prada doing hanging with the Boss?"

EXYOU: It was fun. Until I had to leave.

XIAO HONG: You quit?

EXYOU: The manager wanted to lay off the entire team a few days before Christmas until the first week of the New Year so that they didn't have to pay you for non-working days.

XIAO HONG: I know. They still do.

EXYOU: I sent a letter to the owner telling him I would collect signatures from the people ... and that was my last day. I was fired.

XIAO HONG: Good for you for standing up to them.

EXYOU: I was always causing trouble; asking the manager to raise our wages, complaining about working conditions. Those jerks just want 10% of your brain. If you show them any more than that you're a threat. You can say I'm a bit loud.

XIAO HONG: I'm a bit loud too.

EXYOU: Do you also give the boss a hard time?

XIAO HONG: I would if I could. I barely have enough time to write my articles.

EXYOU: You're a journalist?

XIAO HONG: Well, I'm writing about what happened in my country in Tiananmen Square.

EXYOU: How do you do that from here?

XIAO HONG: We can't do it from there. We tried and thousands of people were killed and many more were sent to jail. That's why I took the night shift at Garbany. I need ninety percent of my brain to make sure the world does not forget about the victims.

EXYOU: You must make your mother worry.

XIAO HONG: She mostly worries about me making her a grandchild.

EXYOU: When parents get old—it's best to only give them the good news.

Beat.

XIAO HONG: Have you been back since?

EXYOU: I'm not ready... Every time my photos were published back home, sniper bullets would hit my house.

XIAO HONG: Why were they after you?

EXYOU: The Serb Militia occupied the mountains around Sarajevo and started spreading bullets and I started taking photos of the mass graves that began flooding the city. Nationalists from every side wanted to separate Serbs, Muslims and Croats to live in separate territories. At the beginning we would joke that the sniper needed new glasses and then it happened.

XIAO HONG: Right.

EXYOU: We were all different fruit in the basket and some

wanted to prove that apple, pear and plum can't be together in the same basket. Fruit is fruit. Yes?

They arrive at the airport.

XIAO HONG: Yes.

Beat.

EXYOU: Here is your stop.

She pays.

Thanks.

XIAO HONG: Thank you.

EXYOU: Say hi to your mother for me.

Scene 10: Word by Word

Offstage: MICHELLE's birthday party. Sounds of drunken singing of "Happy Birthday," noises at a bar, clinking glasses, laughter.

FRIEND 1: Hey Ale, can I get you another?

FRIEND 2: Ale, kiss the birthday girl! C'mon.

ALEJANDRA is haunted by memories of the soldier who tortured her.

SOLDIER: *(Whispers.)* Ale…Ale…Ale

MICHELLE: Where are you going? Ale?!

ALEJANDRA leaves the party. We see her onstage.

ALEJANDRA: It saddens me
to find a woman
with whom I could fall in love
and stay still
pretending that the gag
on my shadow is nothing
trying to make it seem
that it is very common
to live between the cracks
I too could write about gardens
and it would not be difficult to remember
a bouquet of roses
to imagine a different life
a sea long
abandoned to memory

Scene 11: Radio Interview

SEEYYEE is giving a radio interview.

SEEYYEE: Yes well, I've been running all my life. I thought Canada would be where I could stop and catch my breath, where I could look back and see how far I've come. I thought it was a place where I could not only slow down but also settle down and die when my time on earth was up. I saw Canada as my ultimate home away from home.

Now I believe that the world is much wider than Canada. I have become so cynical about nationalisms, even about my own Oromo nationalism. I have come to a place in my life where I will struggle for justice wherever I may be. I want to see myself as a citizen of the world…

We hear but do not see the RADIO HOST.

RADIO HOST: For those of you who have just tuned in we've been talking with our studio guest, Professor Seeyyee Sera, a shining example of a Canadian refugee success story who overcame incredible obstacles in fleeing Ethiopia with her children and found refuge in Canada. Professor Sera will be receiving the Canadian Multi-Cultural Achievement Award tonight at Union Hall.

SEEYYEE: Thank you. I may be in a different space right now but my people are still in bondage and as long as there is suffering in any part of who I am, there will be that deep longing for liberation.

Scene 12: Missing

EXYOU: Longing for language, old friends and graveyards where my family is buried.

ALEJANDRA: My friends, the smell of the bread, my mother's house, the street of my childhood, my language, the mountains, the long conversations in cantinas that never closed, the common utopia, the common struggle, the way people ask you, "How are you doing?" and then they actually stop to hear your answer. The bookstores, the theatres, the music and to sing a song that everybody knows and there is no need for translation.

SEEYYEE: I miss the spirit of resistance, the struggle against oppression. I miss the deeply spiritual connections to the people, to the land, to the flora and fauna. The hubbub of the open market places. The voices of cattle herders calling out as they bring the cattle home from the pastures in the golden glow of the evening sunset. The slippery roads in the rainy season and tripping and falling into the loose mud. I miss my baby brother. I miss the smell of cut grass. I miss the smell of the mouth of a newborn calf…

XIAO HONG: I miss my mother.

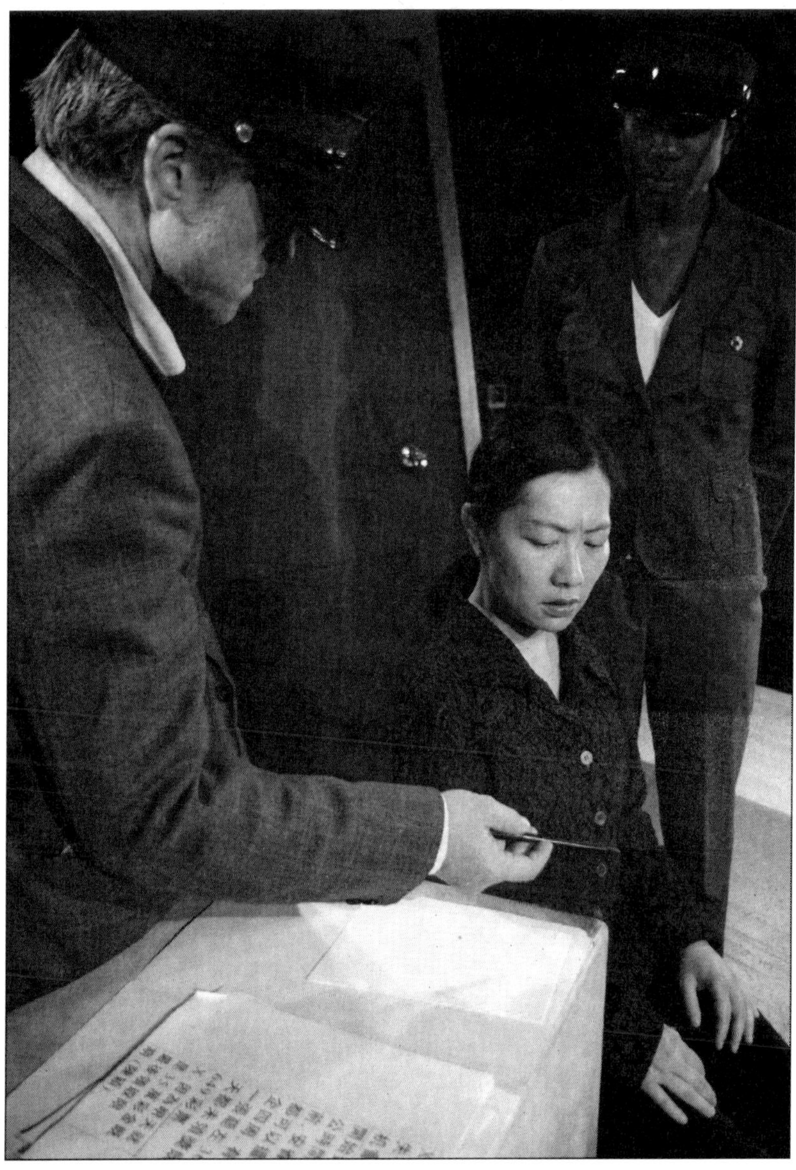

Diana Tso (Xiao Hong) with Interrogators (Patrick Garrow and Miranda Edwards)

Scene 13: Xiao Hong Arrives in Beijing

XIAO HONG arrives at the airport in Beijing. She takes out her passport and gives it to the customs officer. Suddenly security guards surround her and she is arrested.

XIAO HONG: I have a visa. I came back legally.

INTERROGATOR 1: Your name?

XIAO HONG: You have my passport.

INTERROGATOR 1: Wait here.

XIAO HONG: I just want be with my ma for the Mid-Autumn Festival; she is not well; she is waiting for me. I would like to make a phone call to the Canadian Embassy.

INTERROGATOR 1: We are aware of the policy.

XIAO HONG: I've been on a flight for 18 hours. May I please have some water?

INTERROGATOR 2: It would be in the best interest of everyone if you cooperate quickly so you can see your mother and *(Looks at his notes.)* your uncles, Zhang Ying and Zhang Kai.

XIAO HONG: Whatever I have done, I take full responsibility. Do not get my family involved.

INTERROGATOR 2: That is not the way we operate.

XIAO HONG: Oh, so you've been making progress?

INTERROGATOR 1 returns.

INTERROGATOR 1: Take a seat. Was this publication created and distributed by your organization?

XIAO HONG: I just came back to visit my mother.

INTERROGATOR 2: You'll get your chance. Once you answer our questions.

XIAO HONG: You could have me followed day and night, just let me go.

INTERROGATOR 2: You're in no position to be making demands. Tiananmen happened so many years ago, why do you still insist on writing about it?

XIAO HONG: Thousands of people were killed. There were students ground to pieces. How do you expect us to forget?

INTERROGATOR 2: You made China lose face in front of the world. You were a child, swept up in emotional ideas that cost all of us here.

XIAO HONG: I only wrote what I experienced. It was a night of blood, a night of savagery. We didn't have time to run. Fang died in my arms. I swore I would tell the world her story.

INTERROGATOR 2: We must think of our country before ourselves. You didn't understand what was going on.

XIAO HONG: At night I still see the image of her bloodied hair. Our dreams were broken. Our home. Our country.

INTERROGATOR 2: You are living in Canada now. You should write about how Chinese immigrants are discriminated against in Canada, or maybe a romance novel. Or, if you want to see your mother again, write a statement.

The INTERROGATOR shoves a document in her face.

INTERROGATOR 2: You need to acknowledge your mistake. You were foolish. The anti-China powers in the west manipulated you. Write that you deeply regret what you have done. Sign it and promise you will never spread propaganda about the Chinese government again.

INTERROGATOR 1: Write the statement and you can go home to celebrate the Mid-Autumn Festival with your mother tonight. *(Offers her a pen.)*

XIAO HONG doesn't take the pen.

INTERROGATOR 2: Many people have done this. It is not difficult.

XIAO HONG doesn't take the pen.

INTERROGATOR 1: You've been here all day and all night. We can let you go. Take the pen.

XIAO HONG in Mandarin.

XIAO HONG: Ma Ma Wo xiang xin ni neng gou li jie wo, ma wo bu neng qian. *(Translation: Ma, I hope that you can forgive me, Ma, I can't sign it.)*

(To the interrogator.) No.

INTERROGATOR 1: Zhang Xiao Hong is an unwelcome foreigner. Zhang Xiao Hong must be deported to Canada immediately.

Scene 14: Ale's Monologue

ALEJANDRA on the phone with MICHELLE. We hear MICHELLE's voice but do not see her.

MICHELLE: I love you. And this can work, we just have to work at it! Ale? Are you even listening to me?

Beat.

MICHELLE (VO): You do want this, right? Ale?

ALEJANDRA hangs up the phone.

ALEJANDRA: How could I explain to you that even though the scars are not visible it is as if they had amputated my blood, my childhood.

When I talk to myself I do it in Spanish and sometimes I'm not even talking, I'm just repeating words because I like their taste. So I chew words as if they were grapes, almonds, warm bread or raw meat.

I chew them with no haste: llovizna, madrugada, tus manos, barranca, camposanto, tu cintura, hierbabuena, leche tibia, otra vez tus manos, trenes que se van. *(Translation: drizzle, dawn, your hands, ravine, graveyard, your waste, mint, warm milk, your hands once more, trains departing.)*

Sometimes I talk to you while talking to myself and wonder if you ever noticed the constant rain and the trains departing in my poems.

Sometimes I talk to you but I can never find the perfect metaphor or the perfect excuse to explain the endless lumps in my throat, the fog, my orphanage, the tremors…without forgetting the time in which I died over and over under the boots, the fists and the penises of the soldiers who did not understand my silence. Who did not have mercy before my silence.

One of the soldiers put his gun in my mouth and the cold of the metal penetrated my bones almost with the same cruelty of our last kiss this afternoon when I did not know what to say, because I never learned how to say good-bye.

Scene 15: Seeyyee Searches for Words

SEEYYEE is working on her speech for an award she will be receiving. She scribbles something and then erases it. She writes again.

SEEYYEE: I am very happy…flattered…honoured…excited… honoured. I am very honoured to receive this award. The hardest part of adjusting to Canada was when my children finally arrived after four years and we were getting reconnected, more like reestablished…not even reacquainted. We were becoming reacquainted. I was not able to take away the hurts and pains of their childhood. I feel that very profoundly…

I was not able to take away the hurts and pains of my children and become the mother I had always wanted to be. I feel that very profoundly and I continue to search for my lost children every single day of my life. I search for them in the Oromo youth of my community. My brothers and sisters…I search for them in the youth of other communities; I search for them in the youth in the streets… I search…I search for…I search for…hom…

SEEYYEE hears drums from back home.

Baby Brother? Baby Brother? Wait. Wait. Obelaya malo! *(Translation: Brother wait.)*

Miranda Edwards (Seeyee)

Scene 16: Signals

The characters are on a subway. They don't know each other.

SEEYYEE: We
the same ones

EXYOU: we know

ALEJANDRA: we recognize

XIAO HONG: we have traces
of an ill moon under the eyes
and a scent of lonely streets
in our hands

The subway lurches. SEEYEE bumps into XIAO HONG.

SEEYYEE: *(In Oromo.)* Diisuuma… Sorry. *(Translation: Sorry.)*

XIAO HONG: *(Replying to SEEYYEE.)* Sorry.

EXYOU: we don't speak the language
of best-sellers
or trendy bars

SEEYYEE: we move our lips

EXYOU: to

ALEJANDRA: the

XIAO HONG: rhythm

ALEJANDRA: of

EXYOU: a

SEEYYEE: very

XIAO HONG: slow

SEEYYEE: clock

XIAO HONG: that hates and astonishes us

ALEJANDRA: we dance with ghosts

EXYOU: in useless mirrors

ALEJANDRA: we have a scar in our smile

XIAO HONG: and we know how to fold our shadow
in wardrobes

SEEYYEE/
ALE: we

XIAO HONG/
EXYOU: the exiled ones

SEEYYEE: citizens of a nonexistent country

EXYOU: we know
we recognize

XIAO HONG: we walk with tenderness

EXYOU: we have something about death in our gaze.

Scene 17: Haunted

ALEJANDRA enters her basement apartment.

ALEJANDRA: Michelle? Michelle? Are you here?

We hear a crash offstage.

Who's there?! *(Pause.)* Michelle?

The SOLDIER.

SOLDIER: *(Mocking her.)* Michelle! Michelle! Michelle!

ALEJANDRA: Oh. It's you.

SOLDIER: Of course it's me.

ALEJANDRA: Of course. *(Pause.)* Where is she?

SOLDIER: Nice to see you too, Alejandra.

ALEJANDRA: What did you do to her?

SOLDIER: What did I do to her? Me? Maybe I should ask you that question.

ALEJANDRA: What do you mean?

SOLDIER: Look in the bedroom. Go ahead look *(She exits to the bedroom.)* She's gone. Just as you had asked her.

ALEJANDRA reenters.

Isn't that what you wanted?

ALEJANDRA: Of course.

SOLDIER: Isn't that what you asked for?

ALEJANDRA: Yes.

SOLDIER: And so polite about it too. She even made a clean break away. Save for the towel left on the bed. She must have showered before she made her final exit. It's still damp and warm. *(He passes her a note.)* Here. She wanted me to give you this.

She reads it.

There, there. Cheer up. She's safe. Safe from you now. She's probably out somewhere trying to get her mind off you. Doing something weightless and light. That's what everyone else does here.

Long pause.

Don't look so surprised. *(Beat.)* Come on. The food is getting cold. Set the table. *(She does not move.)* Set it. Now.

ALEJANDRA begins to set the table for herself and sits. The SOLDIER looks over her shoulder.

Where is my place here? You know I am always beside you.

ALEJANDRA: I…I didn't mean to hurt her…

SOLDIER: But you did, Ale.

ALEJANDRA: I did but—

SOLDIER: How can she expect to even look into your eyes when we sewed them shut so long ago? Who will unstitch them? You?

ALEJANDRA: My words will unstitch—

SOLDIER: What words, Ale? You never stopped us. Not even a peep. Not a whisper. Not a scream. You remember that. All of you, each and every one of you think that silence is your best weapon. But silence can be misconstrued as compliance.

ALEJANDRA: I need you to leave. I can't have you here. Not tonight.

SOLDIER: You asked me once...you asked me if I remember you, you the girl who howled; the house of flowers that collapsed. Your perverse kisses on my sex that just recently came out of its quarantine. Your silence never stopped us, Ale. Nor the strength in your nails, nor your fucking inability to scream—

ALEJANDRA: NO NO NO.

SOLDIER: NO! I do not remember you. I don't remember you nor any of the thousands. The bodies upon bodies upon which I did the unthinkable. The unthinkable you think of everyday. And yet, here I am, walking beside you always. In the shower, while making love, before you go to sleep. Eating with you always. I am inside you Alejandra. You can never get rid of me...

(l to r): Diana Tso (Old Woman) and Patrick Garrow (Exyou)